Digital Detox

Digital Detox

Clara Wintershade

Contents

1. Introduction to Digital Detox — 1
2. Assessing Your Online Presence — 5
3. Strategies for Digital Detox — 9
4. Mindful Social Media Use — 11
5. Building Healthy Offline Habits — 13
6. Digital Well-being Practices — 17
7. Managing Information Overload — 19
8. Digital Detox and Productivity — 23
9. Maintaining a Balanced Online Presence — 27
10. Digital Boundaries in Relationships — 31
11. Teaching Digital Wellness to Children — 35
12. The Future of Digital Detox — 37
13. Conclusion and Reflection — 39

Copyright © 2024 by Clara Wintershade
All rights reserved. No part of this book may be reproduced in any manner whatsoever without written permission except in the case of brief quotations embodied in critical articles and reviews.
First Printing, 2024

1
Introduction to Digital Detox

Social media and the platforms become an extension of you. They mold to the box they are in. It's almost becoming impossible to tell where someone's offline ends and online presence begins. The digital world moves with them, growing with them – almost. Detoxing is becoming a necessity and an art. More and more people are thinking about their digital legacy: how they appear online, and for how long. To manage your online presence, you need to be vigilant and in control.

More than forty million photos are uploaded to Instagram every day, with two and a half billion "likes". People take ten billion steps every day while using "Fitbit" products. Approximately 50 million people get their news from Twitter. In her 2015 Foreword, Alice Marwick wonders: "Do you spend more hours looking at Facebook or LinkedIn profiles than you do talking face-to-face with the colleagues that sit next to you?" More than you may think. According to the New York Daily News, 38% of people will post to social media at least once before a job interview. A third of them, it adds, checks their profiles every few days. They are updating to build a wired legacy. And maybe become rich, powerful, famous, confident. A first step into taking ownership of these spaces and our feel good/horror stories embedded within them is to develop a healthy relationship with technology.

Understanding the Impact of Technology on Mental Health

In 2022, we know how desperately we need our smartphones. This year saw the Netherlands grind to a halt when a voice system collapse caused Europe's largest port to shut down; Ukrainian authorities warned that Russian cyber-attacks threatened the country's internet, phone systems, and banking. Everywhere, software systems are running the show, from crypto-wallets slipping through regulatory nets to social media algorithms nudging elections. Back in the 1880s when electric light first showed us the limits technology might reach, people worried it was impacting mental health. For many of us in 2022, the thought of an electricity-free existence is itself mystifying. Why, we might be thinking as we scan the news after waking up with an alarm app, should we resist exactly the thing bending so much of our world towards control?

If you worry about your relationship with technology, you're not alone. Your own behavior might be bothering you, or the transformation of spaces you like, or a life-penetrating sense of your own solidities whittling down to ghostly nothing. Many of the technologies we struggle with are social media and smartphones in particular. We are told they provide the networks of safety and connection we need to survive. They hold our attention. But £7 million has been spent on the All-Party Parliamentary Group on Social Media and Young People's Mental Health research, which categorically suggests "social media is causing significant harm to the mental health of young people". Given £5m on researching the negative effects of screen use, the Nuffield Foundation found a 6.6% increase in the percentage of young people who were "at the highest levels of mental health problems" compared with the mid-2000s.

2

Assessing Your Online Presence

Before beginning to develop a digital detox or mindful social media strategies or habits, it can be useful to do an initial self-assessment of your own online presence. It is important to remember that assessing your online presence shouldn't lead to self-blame or guilt. There is no right or wrong online presence. You are unique and trying to change your online presence to model someone else's is unlikely to be sustainable. Instead, take the time to notice how you feel and what you think when you see your online presence as it currently is. What is it about your online presence, including social media, that feels good? What are you proud of when you look at it? What would you like to change? What do you think, really honestly, should remain the same about your online presence? How have you learned about your online behavior after doing this exercise? Do you feel any differently about changing your relationship to social media and online life now that you have assessed what it is already like?

Sharing personal progress on social media can sometimes be a way to help your followers relate to your recovery in a way they may not be able to if you only posted about when you were having tough times, for example. Your self-assessment or reassessment results will help you find your unique answers to these questions. It is this type of reflection, whether it's trying to recover from Cognitive Behavior or trying to have a healthier online life, that can help individuals figure out what they value most about their behavior, what they would like to change, and what they think should remain the same.

Social Media Audit Techniques

In this section, you will learn five different techniques for auditing the way you use social media. Conducting an audit will provide you with critical information about your current use of social media and shed some light on where you can make choices to exercise control over your online presence. Learning about your social media profile will help you evaluate whether or not you need to make changes to your habits.

1. Download your data: Facebook and Google sites provide a way for users to access all the data that has been stored and collected during the time you've been using the platform. 2. Time management: Assess how you manage your time when using social media on your smartphone. Delete social media apps from your phone for an extended period of time or use the built-in 'screen time' functionality to track and limit your social media usage. 3. Find out how data is being used: Facebook, Instagram, and Google provide dashboard-style capabilities to show where data is connected and how it is being used. You may find that ad platforms have created inaccurate or exaggerated profiles of you based on 'data' that has been collected. 4. Determine Facebook tracking: If a network like Facebook is central to your life, then consider opting out of having your actions tracked outside of Facebook (i.e., if you sign into other sites using Facebook). 5. Monitor privacy violations: Data breaches occur all the time and are not just limited to the Facebooks and Instagrams of the world. Sign up for a service like HaveIBeenPwnd to receive notifications

when your data has been exposed to a hack. If a breach happens at a company you use, change your passwords after the fact.

3

Strategies for Digital Detox

Living in the digital age is appealing, but it comes with its disadvantages. We are all tied to our gadgets, whether it is mobile phones, laptops, tablets, desktop computers, or smartwatches. In this scenario, even a few hours disconnected seem like a tough job. However, fear not, as we are here for you and will outline some strategies for digital detox to unplug yourself from excessive and unnecessary use of technology. This approach will help you reclaim your life and shall be a life changer.

The most important thing to keep in mind regarding digital detox is to monitor your technology usage. Keeping an eye on how long you use your phone, laptop, or any other device is something that should be kept on priority. Time management then becomes a pivotal task as once you know the time you spend on digital devices, you will be able to cut down on excessive usage. If you're looking to embrace digital detox and bring more balance to your life, incorporating these strategies can help lay the foundational work for a consistent and real over time. Alongside your commitment to digital detox, be patient with yourself as you move through this journey. Like many things, finding what works best for you is based on finding that balance, something you won't be able to uncover it all... until you give it a try! Don't be too hard on yourself as you navigate this process, and let it be more about progress, as opposed to perfection.

Setting Boundaries with Technology

Creating necessary boundaries with digital consumption, communication, and constantly being connected is a healthy part of a balanced lifestyle. One method of implementing these boundaries into the user's routine is the use of 'tech-resets', which is a part of a digital detox plan. Avoiding overuse of electronics, social media, and entertainment every day helps the user to focus on work, sleep better, communicate with their friends and loved ones more often and more deeply, and be a better parent and friend. Tech resets also contribute to the user's ability to be an active listener. The pacing of communication and the allowance for personal processing of information makes the user's responses, verbal and non-verbal, more reflective and thoughtful.

Understanding that one's technology use is a service to a more balanced, thoughtful life is one way to live proactively, as opposed to merely trying to cut back after more damage has been done. 'Digital detox' is simply taking time to edit the electronic information out of life. This has often been contrasted with simply catching up with calls, emails, texts, and other digital information. Choosing an electronic communications detox day during the weekend can be a nice break for those who have businesses that generally depend on the ebb and flow of email. It is a good idea for people to know on a daily basis that it is possible to reset one's mind in a quiet place where we can gather our thoughts.

4

Mindful Social Media Use

Presently, it is important to explain that there is a growing movement towards "mindful" social media. Many psychologists and neuroscientific experts argue a polyvagal nervous system foundation for these strategies, mostly for digital intervention by indirectly targeting the "social engagement" system. A set of basic and clinical studies have shown the impacts of social media use, and that digital detox and withdrawal are associated with a liberating feel. This emphasis on grounding some form of digital disengagement is an early step toward encouraging more conscious technology utilization. Once a client is mindful and reclaims power over the technology, the approach will continue to help consumers make better choices and develop healthy digital habits.

There is no question about the emphasis our society seems to put on technological savvy. We cannot ignore the rise of smartphones; digital has changed the way we work and entertain ourselves forever, and we cannot even start. But we would argue that a growing number of early adopters of digital intervention programs will find an increasing number of consumers who feel that particular experiences are a beneficial aspect of the patient/client disease education, recovery, and care process. A fundamental problem is that the speed at which digital technology exists makes it very difficult to know the "ideal" number of hours that a customer should use a technological device in a way that is not harmful to their emotional health.

Practicing Digital Mindfulness

Mindful awareness, attention control, and intentionality with digital technology and communication devices lead to digital mindfulness. In this section, specific techniques for cultivating mindfulness in the digital realm are detailed. There are many specific techniques that individuals may use to cultivate mindfulness, and they include a focus on the purpose of a technology, identifying time limits for interacting with the technology and upholding them, and providing social support to act more intentionally with technology. An abundance of research exists on the potential benefits of mindfulness practices for attention, intelligence, and mood. However, technology-laden contexts can become absorbed in these mindful practices. The goal of digital mindfulness is to attend to intentions, decision-making, attention, and connections in online contexts that may be all-consuming.

Returning to the idea of what we want to say, it is possible to be more intentional and less reactive when posting our thoughts in online forums. Having an intention before turning on a computer or smartphone often means that technology serves an individual rather than an individual serving technology. One might choose meditational, contemplative, or relaxing practices earlier in the day in order to inform optimal use of technology later in the day. Giving oneself permission to not check emails or respond to messages in a timely fashion can be another way of taking control of electronic media. Having alternative activities and hobbies that do not involve a screen help to balance one's exposure to technology. Technology boundaries are ways of taking more control over work and personal time management.

5

Building Healthy Offline Habits

Live in the moment - Sometimes, it is okay to just be without capturing and uploading everything. It is crucial to take time off from app notifications and alert systems. It's okay to let it sit. Try and relax and calm down in the real world.

Transportation turn off - Whenever possible, turn off or put on silent mode your phone while at public transportation, be it library, church, checking in at the movie theatre, or buying groceries. Do you really need your phone at that time?

Take the scenic route - What can be more enjoyable than taking a leisurely walk through a new neighborhood when traveling or experiencing a sunny day? Stop and smell the roses when you can. Put down your phone and consider visiting the essentials of your area.

Routine technical turn off - Desired evenings in quiet are necessary. Turn off your computer at a reasonable time and limit your contact with your devices, ensuring you have a relaxed space to work. The weekend should not be used to catch up with work, although this is not possible for certain jobs or lifestyles.

Avoid relationship ruts - Stop blaming digital networks, check-in at a trendy bar and schedule a friendly evening for the day with your friends.

Go offline - Going offline should be your digital detox plan. Your vacation is your time, use it as an opportunity to lead your life. Allocate a small amount of time to verify your social status each day, having the majority of your time offline. Fitting healthy routines into your routine is fine whether it's coffee with a close friend, calling or doing things online for a day of good friends. If you have Instagram open or have an endless scroll on Twitter it's almost possible to get another 'hit' in a dopamine rush from our 'reward center' when we see that the number of likes we got has crept up. Any funny insights in the message?

Engaging in Offline Activities

Unplugging—disconnecting from the online world—is not, however, merely about turning off. While it may, of course, include abandoning your screen, the deep and beneficial message at its core is emphatically and positively engaging with offscreen experiences. A cultural acknowledgment that a world without the internet and social media would represent a better place merely attempts to retrieve a sense of what has been left behind because it now so acutely incorrect. Detoxing is really about engaging in a range of experiences you love and, by doing so, becoming interested—indeed, absorbed is a better word—through these experiences. Creating a plan and seeking out the practices and places that make up those everyday quadrants—agency, communion, age, and wonder—could form the foundation for a life of digital detoxing that doesn't seem quite so... digital.

The aim is to show how it is possible to orient oneself in a way that considers technology as a sufficient meditative agent—meaning it is significantly gratifying as a tool. One of the hallmarks, then, we might suggest of a life that is mindful of possibilities of digital detoxing is that it is cognizant of their broader non-digital milieu. "The Internet ceases to be a digital problem," as Turkle writes, "when we think about it in the context of our entire life." Paid as invisible, which is to say truly powerful. In essence, digital detoxing is possible, but it can't involve a sneaky or monopolizing asceticism that demands rekindling with life by scorning the nonvirtual. The way to suffer less in an over-mediated society is to discover lights, through work, that inspire us and by extension improve the wider environments they filter into. A digital detox, for instance, is already active in many Open Work environments given their support of connectivity and also the provision of spaces free to all workers who seek some offline time.

6

Digital Well-being Practices

Digital well-being practices encourage a range of activities with regard to media use: from resetting boundaries around what is shared online, to unplugging entirely during periods of rest. These outlined guidelines set the stage for social media use that is mindful, intentional, and healthy. It is not enough to instruct students on professional best use of social media or privacy concerns; a more ethical and whole-person approach is advocated in these guidelines. By working toward and modeling greater awareness of digital well-being, we not only break down the myth of the 24/7 connected academic but also encourage further debate, as the values that are important to us are continually negotiated in our home and professional lives.

Summary of Digital Well-being Practices

- Setting Priorities: Focus on the well-being of the body, mind, and soul above and beyond constant media monitoring. - Practicing Privacy Self-awareness: Be aware of which media we use to discuss particular topics and know who could potentially view these communications. - Unplug Regularly: Establish periods of rest where we unplug and are not in constant communication.

Cultivating a Healthy Relationship with Technology

We are not masters of our technological devices. In many cases, these machines are either sapping away our attention or becoming a permanent, addictive part of our lives. There are some practical things that we can do to foster a healthy relationship with our technologies. Although these small changes in behavior will not entirely solve the problem, they can help to promote a sense of digital well-being and mindful usage.

One big source of addiction and distraction for young people today is social media. However, although many people feel like they are distracting themselves from social media as much as ever, the stats suggest they may be moving away from these platforms. Twitter has struggled to add new users for a while, and its user numbers have actually been dropping for the past four quarters. On Facebook, we have seen significant drops in engagement metrics among the most prolific users. Maybe people are finally realizing that these platforms are primarily motivated by profit margin rather than human connection.

7
Managing Information Overload

We live in an era of digital transformation and heavy information consumption. The average person consumes 100,000 words of information in a single day – equivalent to Moby Dick! A 2009 University of California, San Diego paper estimated that in 2008, Americans consumed information for about 12 hours per day, or about 100,500 words, outside of work. The average worker receives 300 emails per week, which requires 1 hour of sorting and decision-making per day. Since then, many advances have been made in the digital and information world and this number has likely increased.

In the wake of this content explosion, successful online users use filters and routines to protect their time and keep abreast of the most important subjects. Some well-known tricks to focus in a world of unfiltered data include: not checking inboxes and social media first thing in the morning, blocking out reading time and email time, and using services such as Pocket or Evernote to keep track of interesting articles. Managing the flow of new information is important in a comprehensive digital detox, and information convenience is directed at an important piece of that – but it is only one piece. Research has shown that not only do people feel overloaded because of the new, filtered information that is coming in, they also feel overloaded because of what they might be missing while they're offline. In the same way people have turned to cleanses and detoxes as a temporary diet solution, some people are turning to digital detoxes to manage the constant flow of email, messages, likes, favorites, pokes, tweets, Instagrams, and more, and opt out for a while.

Effective Information Filtering Techniques

This chapter offers an ample list of techniques for knowing about and filtering the vast amount of information that is content of our digital everyday life. We explore these mechanisms that allow us to manage content overload and to filter information before it is fed to the plethora of algorithms that categorize, discard, and select information for us. The bulk of this filter activities is done based on traceable behavioral patterns in information search and studies are impressive in uncovering not only the tiny scale of attention during news consumption, but also the psychological and cultural impact of such a privacy and custom-tailored bit of attention to receptor informational routines. This section is written as a hands-on guideline to filter for the common user. Laurie Penny, for instance, suggests less technologically radical, yet still feasible ways in which your readers can hide in the gap - limiting their Facebook searches and imposed friendings to certain thresholds, focusing on every time they interacted online, researching what "web beacons" are and using Tor.

It aims for practical methods which still amount to a 'manual' grace, bits of personal computer wizardry which apply technology, but too content. Therefore, in the following pages, when referring to techniques for managing digital excess, we will focus on certain surveillance evasion tactics which are particularly effective for minimizing creeping information overload and social-media saturation. Information filtering is important not just in the noble cause of unpredictably staggering the flow of data through network silos and interactions, but to preserve attention. While alternative information propagation models reduce the surfing power of elite groups of receptors, they require large-scale changes outside of common alternatives for the vast majority. To stop ourselves from finding out too much faster about social or digital activity that lead to conspicuous connections, which could have a tangible increasing exhaustion and un-thought, we propose: use safe searching. Filter or a-hack surpluses on the infrastructure side.

8

Digital Detox and Productivity

The 21st century has made a lot happen in terms of technology, innovations, and trends. It's no surprise that platforms' designs are intentionally addictive to form a strong bond with the users. The social media trends and content suggestions are designed to hook individuals into unproductivity and keep up with active engagement on social media platforms, browsing random videos, liking, sharing, and endlessly scrolling! Being aware of the psychological effects of digital stimuli, individuals today are into strategies that focus on disconnection from digital media known as "Digital Detox" practices. The digital detox is a great way to gain improved mental and emotional well-being.

We live in a world that is driven by the digital era, and it's nearly impossible to bypass the internet. However, it has its negative effects in terms of enhancing efficiency in life. If you are glued to your screens or digital media for hours, it can adversely impact your role as an employee. There are very specific studies and research that show the linkage between having a digital detox and improved productivity that comes with it. It's a great way to eradicate a major amount of stress and disconnect yourself temporarily from the overly indulgent digital world. There are even certain benefits of digital detox, like having better focus and concentration. It helps you declutter the basics and can manage tasks effectively. The focus gets better, and the concentration improves greatly once we tend to take to the disappearing act of the digital detox practices. This improvement is very necessary for a boost to the productivity of the employees.

Improving Focus and Concentration

Of course it is difficult to concentrate when surrounded by or immersed in distractions, and this problem becomes more prevalent with increasing amounts of digital noise. This is why attention is a key ability developing in the quest for cognitive enhancement and ultimately the higher achieved SMARTER mind. The primary method to improve basic attentional skills is concentration meditation; this typically involves trying to focus upon one specific thing, such as a candle flame, one's breathing, or a repeated sound. Concentration meditation is also found in other traditions, such as yoga, where the chosen object is often a mantra (a repeated word or phrase that is silently spoken in the mind). A simple method to refocus and start a mental break is to perform a short stretch and maybe take a walk around the office.

One simple technique is to incorporate regular planned relaxation breaks; brief diversions for the mind are built into the SMARTER resting principle, and in turn these regular mental minibreaks restore attention, improve clarity and release tension. A short even shift of a person's attention away from a problem they may be experiencing will put them in a better situation to solve the cognitive problem. Not only is it important for an individual's mental ability to take the mind off a problem as it reduces stress and allows a person to think about the problem sensibly rather than make hasty decisions, regular breaks can also lead to better work overall and an improvement in health, as stress can be a cause of illness. By remembering to take these regular mental breaks at the same time each day, behavior can be modified.

9

Maintaining a Balanced Online Presence

Digital well-being allows you to maintain a balance in your digital life, one that isn't all-consuming or anxiety-producing. It's the expert recommendation for a healthy relationship with digital technologies. Following that same pattern, it's a good idea to set intentions for your social media presence and activities as well.

Here are some steps you can use to create a personalized social media plan:

1. Define your intent: What is the purpose of your digital activities? What do you hope to gain and give while you are engaged in them? Asking yourself these questions helps to give your activities direction and help keep things in perspective. Is the positive stuff worth any negative impacts you may feel? Why or why not? How might you mitigate the negative impacts while still holding on to some of the positive impacts of the activity, or consider whether to still look into quitting your digital activity?

2. Create a healthy online presence. Evaluate whether your actual online presence (based on your activities) is an accurate representation of who you believe you are offline (in-person). Try to promote

and maintain a healthy and realistic representation of who you believe you are.

3. Social media and personal "digital branding" is also one feature of cultivating one's online presence. Sharing your online activities can tell the rest of the world who you are to varying degrees.

4. Determine how you'll integrate social media use. Define the social media main activity pattern(s) which you will use to meet your intentions or greater meaning (i.e., alignment with availability): - Posting about events or items in my own life (e.g., status updates, re-tweeting news items of interest to you) - Following along with interesting focusing and unique groups, topics, or circles of friends - Re-tweeting or otherwise sharing relevant social media content; possibly including kid and parental advice/news items by others - Other

SIGNIFICANT tip: Unsubscribe from the feeds in which you would like to limit or alter your behavior (i.e., the main activity patterns in which people engage you in).

Creating a Personalized Social Media Plan

Creating a personalized social media plan

It is time to take hold of the reins of your social media usage and engagement, far beyond detailed how-to's for closing down the most common accounts. Even if you do not plan on deactivating an account or closing out an email address, this section has something for you because it is focused on the past and present of your online engagement. To start your journey with social media wellness, take possession of a sheet of paper or a blank word processor file. If you would like to give a printout of this lesson a try, you have 6 pages of content ahead of you. You may want to keep a copy of that on your computer in the event you accidentally lose the hard copy.

Downtime to Detox: What to Write

That page for note-taking is now a Success Section. A Success Section is where you, as a bold act of defining them head-on, write down as many ideas as possible that will motivate, inspire, teach, and help you at some point in the future. As of now, we have been discussing and completing a series of pages all about social media management, but yours might very well be about drug prescriptions, business ideas, sewing patterns, or anything at all that matters to you personally. So if you have anything in your head that might be considered an asset, be sure to write that down. That sheet is the home of the notes, so grab a writing tool or tap at the keys. Write, text, draw, sketch, doodle, scribble, twiddle, or tiddle. This is your time, and therefore your space.

10

Digital Boundaries in Relationships

Digital presence and social media must be engaging for more than just personal self-care; it is equally important in personal relationships. When in a partnership, cohabiting, dating, or married, creating boundaries within the digital environment is a healthy practice.

Setting digital boundaries in any relationship is directly related to how we feel about our personal digital well-being. It is equivalent to discussing financial, homeownership, parenting, car-sharing, and grocery shopping goals. Approaching one's digital presence is a point of conversation and a space where respect, trust, and security can be decided upon. To bring it up, Ariel Anders, MSW, therapist and relationship educator at the University of Washington, shares that communication of this issue can begin in several ways. Following a discussion of technology boundaries in the relationship, the next step is to create a technology agreement. This agreement will embody the digital boundaries and bring clarity to the relationship. This digital agreement will save time and energy, Anders explains, "processing regret and repairing after a mistake is easier and more respectful if your boundary is written down ahead of time." The technology agreement and established digital norms can save the hurt feelings that come with broken promises related to technology. Further, if a partner has a hard time communicating or understanding technology utilization in the relationship, Anders recommends outside professional individual and/or couple's therapy.

You must be clear and firm in your actions. If your partner is unable to be responsive or uninterested in creating a balanced technology usage pattern, strong consideration for ending the relationship should be a consideration. Social media and digital presence are common relationship tools that can add value and/or destruction. As such, it is imperative to fully consider taking responsibilities for stepping out of the digital world.

Communicating Boundaries with Others

Digi, as a system, details all of the infrastructural, corporate, institutional, and interpersonal dynamics intersecting in one's everyday digital tool use and deployment. Digi includes a comprehensive toolset of strategies to digitally detox and strategically reintroduce an individual back into the digital ecosystem. Digi, as a practice, asks users to communicate openly with others about their needs and expectations for how they will be a part of their life in this way. While these strategies speak to individuals, a large part of the practice of Digi is focused on navigating the people in your life. By giving folks 'communication backlog homework,' we ask emergent Digi users to carefully and thoughtfully consider the conversations they need to have with others about their recent break and their plans to move forward. In this way, we offer a basis for a communal intervention aimed at giving people the space to change alongside the tools to actually realize and become those changes.

The recommendation here is to allow for a digital detox as many times as an individual needs it and to be generous and loving in how others are welcomed back into one's life – as many times as they need it. If one can't hold these boundaries over time, it may mean that the relationship is no longer healthy for the individual. Your hope is in initiating a discussion that frames your detour from your shared digital labyrinth of stress and exhaustion as a time not just needed but needed by your friend, needed by your community, needed by the wider world.

11

Teaching Digital Wellness to Children

The new CPS report sets out principles for good practice in developing digital wellness practitioners and programmes, and teaching it in education settings, based on expert opinion, an insight event, and a review of digital wellness programmes. "We know how we want our children to treat their friends in the playground, and this extends online too," says Ms. Falconer. "We should sing out positively in our own lives about the joys of being offline as well as online."

Digital well-being and social good health is vital for improving children's outcomes. There is a growing field of expertise in digital wellness, which can illuminate best practice. Specifically, the principles of digital wellness that a child should master are well-being, self-worth, self-control, respect, nurturing friendships, and mindfulness. These would combine into managing screens and platforms, and setting boundaries and showing empathy. The role of adults in young children managing their online time is a burdensome responsibility and an obligation. Parents and other adults need to be clear in their own minds that they are good role models for their children in their internet use, and show them the maximum empathy and understanding possible. "We also need to create a nation of citizens who express conscious and responsible publishing across digital platforms, and understand and respond to the digital footprint they are leaving," says Ms. Falconer. Essentially, this approach underlines digital well-being skills for life – ethical, socially responsible habits; emotional robustness; controlling the digital landscape rather than having it control the individual – and so ultimately brings social as well as individual good health and well-being.

Educating Kids on Healthy Tech Habits

Activity Stuff Educating Kids on Healthy Tech Habits The baggage and carryover from the pandemic into our digital lives is familiar for kids, too. For many, time with technology and social media peaked as avenues for staying connected and being part of their peer circles. The allure of likes, posts, and popular threads added to the draw, sapping the intent of un-commented screen period. Shifting gears can be met with mixed reception. Here are some ideas for creating an approach and conversation for this new venture. Kids often don't get opportunities to gauge the consequences of their online self and how that affects others. It's really important to talk about this.

Practicing Skills Encourage them to post an activity with their non-dominant hand or a family outdoor game with a selfie using a silly Snapchat lens. Find a few different tutorials for a fun action, like making an ice cream cone, doing the floss, or showing off a different sport trick. Post the video with space for comments by peers to tell which one they think is the best or more interesting.

12

The Future of Digital Detox

The future of digital unwell-being and digital detox will likely be determined by the fortunes of four trends: luxury resort retreats and exotic adventures, meditation and mindfulness, internet regulations and restrictions, and algorithmic control by Big Tech. The future of digital detox and digital well-being presents itself as alternating between exotic privation in paradise and deep absorption in inward-looking contemplation. The evolution of any one of these four directions and the various innovations within them will be at least partially determined by how external circumstances dictate.

The retreats of tomorrow will still offer a return to an earlier, purer time, even if that earlier, purer time is predominantly fictional. They will also be more luxurious, more exotic, more orientalized. The innovation behind them in ten years' time will not be just the same old ten-day silent Vipassana retreat in rural Sweden, but the ten-day silent Vipassana 'surprise' club break... in Colombo, Sri Lanka. In the far future, the places to which people will go on digital detox may not exist during any one time, but will instead be animated by tourist charters, with their photogenic ruins of 21st-century infrastructure. These guided excursions will bear out the ultimate end of digital disconnection and the ultimate EdTech anti-utopia. Up that rotten scaffold the brave new world they walk.

Emerging Trends in Digital Well-being

Evolving nature and emerging trends. As emerging trends in technology and digital well-being intersect to form a field of digital well-being research, there is an opportunity to anticipate the advancements that might be made by scholars and practitioners. Against this backdrop, we outline some of the practices that may become future potential foci of research, exploring the practices and pitfalls of digital well-being and suggesting a trajectory for these initiatives that place more emphasis on individual, consumer-facing strategies. In the following section, a thorough review of these topics and issues is offered within the primary literature on digital detox.

Focusing and refocusing practices. It is worthwhile considering not only resistive tactics against the encroachment of digital technologies and the discontent they bring, but also practices that incorporate the digital. Research in this direction is in its early stages. Many of the programs, apps, and even the general sentiment towards the pursuit of what is labeled "digital well-being" continue to be primarily or even exclusively concerned with the negative effects of exposure to screen-based activities, especially social media consumption. The future trajectory of these initiatives, clearly related to the broader development of positive interventions in positive computing, could allow for increasingly personalized consumer goods designed around "digital well-being", from technologies used for managing online presence such as MyPersonality, to preventive and responsive strategies aimed at reducing the 'pain' of a break-up on Facebook, in the furthering of combined efforts by industry leaders to promote digital well-being.

13

Conclusion and Reflection

Send off - To finally conclude, after reflecting on technology and how it fits into my life, I am happy to say that I am confident that I can maintain a digital detox. I am mindful and intentional about being present in my personal life. I am also aware of my online presence and how it represents the woman that I am. With the use of a daily journal, I hope to consistently follow the plan I have laid out for myself. Moreover, I can eagerly say that I am beyond excited to dedicate a day to digital detox next week. Using that 24-hour period, I can zone in and focus on myself rather than the messages pinging from my phone. I am excited to take this time and come back with a refreshed mind and a clear statement as to whether a digital detox is feasible for me.

Incorporating feedback is an essential trait that I possess, and actively do on a daily basis. My peers have given me great insight as to how and why it is important to use a digital detox. Furthermore, the feedback I received made me think about the potential pitfalls of a digital detox. The peer feedback highlighted topics that were significant to the overall impact of my essay. My classmates were able to pinpoint topics to explore further. Additionally, my peers were able to provide me with a list of topics to explore or questions to answer. This feedback is useful for two reasons: I am able to receive different perspectives on the material of my essay, yet I am also able to organize the essay in a new manner. I think receiving this feedback has allowed me to make a handful of revisions to my project proposal. Ultimately, this essay takes into consideration not only the original proposal but also the feedback suggestions.

www.ingramcontent.com/pod-product-compliance
Lightning Source LLC
LaVergne TN
LVHW041641070526
838199LV00052B/3484